Cambridge English Readers

Level 1

Series editor: Philip Prowse

Parallel

Colin Campbell

CAMBRIDGE UNIVERSITY PRESS
Cambridge, New York, Melbourne, Madrid, Cape Town, Singapore,
São Paulo, Delhi, Dubai, Tokyo

Cambridge University Press
The Edinburgh Building, Cambridge CB2 8RU, UK

www.cambridge.org
Information on this title: www.cambridge.org/9780521536516

First published 2003
5th printing 2010

Printed in China by Sheck Wah Tong Printing Press Limited

A catalogue record for this publication is available from the British Library

ISBN 978-0-521-53651-6 Paperback
ISBN 978-0-521-68613-6 Book with Audio CD Pack

Contents

Prologue *An underground station in London*

The tall young woman walked down the platform and then stopped. It was six o'clock in the evening and there were a lot of people waiting for the train. A man in a black suit walked down the platform and stopped two or three metres from the woman.

A train came into the station. The woman turned and looked at it. The man came and stood behind her. He put his hand on her back. She turned and looked at him. There was a question on her face. Her mouth and eyes opened wide. He pushed her hard. He heard nothing. Only the train. The woman fell in front of it.

The next day in the newspapers:

WOMAN DIES UNDER TRAIN

Chapter 1 *The first phone call*

Three years later

The young woman answered the phone.

'Julie.' It was her father.

'Dad. Where are you?'

'I'm outside the station. I'm going to get him.'

'Now?'

'Yes.'

'Dad, are we doing the right thing? Is this right?'

'Julie, we talked about this.'

'I know but now . . . I'm just not sure this is the right thing.'

'Remember our conversation, Julie. We made our decision. We have to do this.'

Chapter 2   *A visitor*

It was late and it was getting dark. Max sat in the bedroom of his flat. He lived in London and the noise of cars outside never stopped. But now he didn't hear the noise. He sat on his bed. There was a gun on the bed beside him. The gun was still warm. Max's face was very white and he didn't feel well.

He never felt well after he killed someone. He sat in the dark flat with his head against the wall. His eyes were closed. But then slowly, he opened them. Someone was outside his flat. He didn't hear anything, but he knew. He knew someone was there. He stood up and took the gun from the bed. He walked to the window and looked out. Cars went by. He saw a white car. It was a police car, but it didn't stop. There weren't many street lights and it was dark now. But he could see there was no one in the street. No policemen. No one.

He listened. There was still no noise. But someone was there, he knew it. Some things he always knew.

He walked to the door. There was a small television above the door and he looked up at it. There was a man outside his front door – a tall man in an expensive suit. Max could see the man's face very well, but he didn't know him. Max put the gun in the back of his trousers and opened the door.

'Max Holland?'

'Yes.'

'My name's Gerald Fairhead. Can we talk?'

'What about?'

'I've got a job for you, Max.'

'I'm not looking for work, Mr Fairhead.'

'I can give you a lot of money.'

'I don't need money, Mr Fairhead. Good night.'

Max started to close the door.

The man put his hand on the door. 'I've got something else for you,' the man said, 'some photographs. Some very interesting photographs for you.'

'Photographs of what?'

The man moved his hand towards his pocket. Max hit him. He hit him once. He hit him hard. Just below the chin. The man fell to the floor.

Chapter 3   *Photographs*

Max stood for a minute and listened. There was no noise. He brought Fairhead into the flat and closed the door. Fairhead didn't move. Max put his hand in the man's pocket. There was no gun. But he felt something. He took out some photographs and walked to the window. He turned on a light and looked at one of the photographs. It was a photograph of a priest, standing outside a church. He looked at a second photograph and then a third and then a fourth. The same man was in all the photographs.

Max looked carefully at the priest's face. Then he quickly looked at all the photographs again. Fairhead started to move. Max turned to look at him. Fairhead sat up slowly and started to speak.

'Why . . . why did you . . . ?'

He didn't finish the question.

Max spoke, 'I thought you had a gun in your pocket, but you didn't. I didn't know that. In my job, I have to be careful.'

Fairhead looked at the photographs in Max's hand.

'You found them,' he said.

'What are these, Mr Fairhead? Why did you come here? Why did you bring these photographs?'

'Don't you know the face, Max? It's *you*. It's *your* face.'

'What are you talking about?'

'It's the other Max Holland. Max Holland the priest.'

Chapter 4   *The job*

'Why did you come to see me, Mr Fairhead?' Max asked.

'I told you. I have a job for you. I want you to do something for me and I can give you a lot of money.'

'What's the job, Mr Fairhead?'

'Your usual kind of job, Max. You see, I have a problem.'

'What's his name? The name of your problem.'

'*Her* name,' said Fairhead.

Max looked at him coldly.

'A woman?' he asked.

'Yes. Is that a problem for you, Max? I know you kill women.'

Max said nothing.

Fairhead spoke again, 'This woman, my problem, she works for an important newspaper. And she knows something about me. I don't want her to write about me in her newspaper.'

'What does she know about you?'

'I'm a careful man too, Max. I'm not going to tell you that.'

'Why don't you give her some money?'

'I can't buy this woman, Max. But I can buy you.'

'And these?' Max had the photographs in his hand. 'Where did you get them? This is *my* face. You put *my* face in these photographs. Why?'

'The photographs are real, Max. This is a real man. He

looks like you, his name's also Max Holland and he's a priest. I can take you to meet this other Max.'

'I don't understand. What are you saying? Who is he? Why does he look like me?'

'Good questions, Max. I can answer them, but it's going to be difficult to understand.'

'I can understand most things, Mr Fairhead.'

'Well, Max. This man is you. But he doesn't live in this world.'

Chapter 5 *Parallel worlds*

'What do you mean? He doesn't live in this world?' Max asked.

'I told you this isn't going to be easy, Max. You see, you live in London, and this man lives in London, but they're not the same Londons. They're parallel Londons. There are many parallel Londons, and many parallel Madrids, and Tokyos and Istanbuls . . . there are many parallel worlds.'

'Parallel worlds? What are you talking about, Mr Fairhead?'

'Listen, Max. I know it's difficult to understand, but there are many, many worlds, not just this one. And in every one of these worlds there's a Max Holland and a Gerald Fairhead. The same people. The same people but . . . they're a little different.'

'What are you talking about? The same but different?'

'Well Max, look at this man in the photographs. He's Max Holland too. He's the same Max Holland as you but . . . he's a little different from you.'

'What do you mean, the same?'

'He comes from Manchester. Just like you. His father's name was John and his mother's name was Mary. Just like yours. He had a sister called Joanne. Just like you. And his father, mother and sister died. Just like your parents and sister.'

Max stood up and walked over to Fairhead. He took the gun from the back of his trousers.

'You know a lot about me, Mr Fairhead. I don't like that. No one knows this much about me. Are you going to tell me who you are? Or am I going to kill you?'

'I do know a lot about you and I know a lot about this man,' Fairhead replied. 'Don't you want to meet him? Don't you want to meet the other you?'

Max looked at Fairhead. 'Can you take me to this man?' he asked.

'Yes, I can take you to him. I can take you to this other world. You can see him, then you can do my job for me,' Fairhead answered.

Max looked at the gun in his hand and then at Fairhead.

Fairhead smiled at him, 'I know what you're thinking, Max, and you're right. You can kill me at any time. So, you've got nothing to lose. Come with me.'

Chapter 6 *Different decisions*

Max put the gun on the table.

'These different worlds. How . . . ?' He didn't finish the question. He looked at Fairhead and then at the photographs he still had in his hand. 'I don't understand, Mr Fairhead. Different worlds? Why? Why are there parallel worlds?'

'Every day Max, we make decisions. Lots of decisions. Little decisions, big decisions. To get up in the morning or to stay in bed; to walk to work or to take the bus; to phone someone or not to phone someone. Our decisions make a difference to our lives. They make a difference to other people's lives, and they make a difference to the world we live in. I'll give you an example. A woman is out walking. She hears some music. She walks towards the music and sees some people singing. The woman stops and asks a man about the music. They talk, they laugh. They meet again. They fall in love. You see? All the little decisions she made – to go for a walk, to stop and ask this man about the music. All these decisions made a big difference to her world. There are other worlds where the woman goes for a walk, but doesn't stop and doesn't talk to a man.'

Fairhead stopped for a minute and looked at Max. He was listening carefully.

Fairhead spoke again, 'And there are parallel worlds where there are different Max Hollands. They made different decisions and they're different people. The same, but different.'

Fairhead stopped speaking and looked at Max. Max said nothing. He walked to the window and looked out.

'So what are you saying, Mr Fairhead? There are other worlds with different Max Hollands? Max Hollands who made different decisions from me?'

'Yes.'

Max laughed. 'That's very interesting. I like it. But the question is, are you right?'

'Come and see, Max. Come and see.'

Chapter 7 *Going to another world*

Max stood and looked at Fairhead for some time. He didn't speak. He looked down at the photographs in his hand, then he looked up at Fairhead. He made his decision.

He took the gun from the table. 'Take me to this other world, but remember – I can kill you. I can kill you any time I want.'

Fairhead smiled, 'Of course, Max. Of course.'

They left the flat and walked down the street. They didn't speak. After five minutes they stopped outside an underground station.

Max laughed. 'We're going to a parallel world by train!'

'Yes,' Fairhead answered, 'but it's a different kind of train.'

They walked into the station. Fairhead walked up to a lift door and pressed the button.

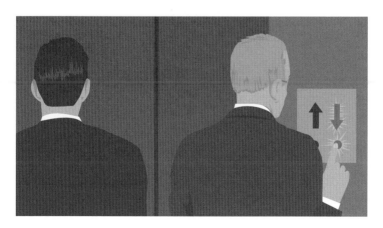

The doors opened. Fairhead walked into the lift and Max followed him. The doors closed and the lift started to go down. It went down and down. For three minutes, four minutes, five minutes.

The lift stopped and the doors opened. They were on a platform but it was empty. There were no people.

'What do we do now, Mr Fairhead?' Max asked.

'We wait, Max. We wait for a train,' Fairhead answered. 'Do you like travelling by train, Max? Do you like underground stations?'

Max looked at him. 'Why do you ask?'

Fairhead didn't answer. 'I think I can hear a train, Max,' he said. He turned and put his hand on Max's back.

'Don't do that!' Max said and pushed the hand away.

'Did she fall Max, or did you push her?' Fairhead asked.

'What are you talking about, *her*? Who are you talking about?'

'The woman, Max. The woman. Did she fall in front of the train or did you push her?'

'You know too much about me, Mr Fairhead.'

'Yes Max, but I'm not going to tell anyone. You do this job for me and I won't tell anyone about you.'

The train came into the station and stopped. There was no one on it. They got on. The train started. It started slowly, but then went faster. The lights went out. It was very dark. The train went faster.

Chapter 8 *Another London*

The train stopped. The doors opened and the lights came on. Max and Fairhead got off the train. They were on another empty platform. Max looked around. There was no station name. There were no pictures on the walls. There was nothing at all.

Fairhead walked down the platform and then stopped in front of another lift.

'Are you coming, Max?' he said.

Max followed him into the lift. Fairhead pressed the button and the lift started to go up.

'Lifts look the same in your world,' Max said.

'Not everything is different,' Fairhead replied, 'but not everything is the same. Wait and see.'

The lift doors opened. They stood and looked at the street.

'It doesn't look like a different world,' Max said.

They walked out of the lift. Fairhead started to walk down the street, but Max stood and looked around for a minute. Then he followed Fairhead.

'Do you know where we are, Max?' Fairhead asked.

'No, I don't. Where are we?'

Fairhead didn't answer. He walked on.

Max looked up. The street lights were very strong so he looked down again quickly. He looked around. There were no cars on the street, no buses, nothing. Then Max saw someone walking on the other side of the street. The man stopped when he saw Max. Then he turned and ran back down the street.

'What's wrong with him?' Max asked.

'This London isn't very safe, Max,' Fairhead said. 'Not many people go out at night. Look around you. Everything is closed. Everything. The restaurants, the bars, the shops, everything is closed. People don't go out at night. That man saw you looking at him. I think he was afraid of you.'

'The street lights are really strong here,' Max said.

'The police like to see everything – they watch everyone day and night. People don't feel afraid with strong lights at night.'

'The strong lights make the night look like day,' Max said.

'It's a different London, Max. We're in a parallel world.'

Chapter 9 *The woman's house*

'This is where she lives, Max.'

They were in a small street two or three minutes from the station.

'Which house?' Max asked.

'Number nine.'

'Does she live with anyone?' Max asked.

'No, she doesn't.'

Max looked up and down the street. 'It's quiet. That's good.'

'So, are you going to do it? Are you going to do the job?'

'After I see *him*, Mr Fairhead. First you take me to see . . . to see this other Max Holland, and then we can talk about your job.'

'No. We're not going to *talk* about the job. You're going to *do* the job. I'm going to take you to see the priest now. Then you come back here and do the job,' said Fairhead.

'I could kill you now,' replied Max.

'I know, but you want to see him. You want to know why he's different. You want to know why he's a priest and you're a killer.'

Max didn't answer. Fairhead smiled. He knew he was right.

'Good. I'm going to take you to him now. You can talk to him and you can ask him why you're different. But meet me back at the station in two hours. After you . . . finish the job.'

Chapter 10 *The second phone call*

'Julie?'

'Yes.'

'I'm back,' the man said.

'Did he come with you?' the woman asked.

'Yes, he's here.'

'Is he with you now?'

'No, he went to see the priest.'

'When are you coming here, Dad?' the woman asked.

'Now. I'm coming now.'

'Dad.'

'Yes.'

'What's he like?'

'He's a killer, Julie. Don't forget that. You don't need to know anything more about him.'

Chapter 11 *Meeting in a church*

The church was cold. There were two or three candles, but it was still dark. Max looked around. There was no one there. He stood at the back and waited. Then a door at the front of the church opened and the priest walked in. The priest turned to the front and then sat down. Max walked quietly to the front of the church. The priest heard nothing. Max sat down behind the priest. They sat without speaking for a minute or two. The priest didn't move.

'Don't turn around. Don't move.'

The priest started to turn but then stopped. 'Can I help you?' he asked.

Max knew the voice. It was his voice.

'I want to ask you a question,' Max said.

'Of course. Come and sit here with me and we can talk.'

'No. We can talk like this.'

'Do I know you?' the priest asked.

'No, you don't know me. You don't know me at all,' Max answered. 'But I have a question for you. Why did you become a priest?'

'Why did I become a priest?'

'Yes. Why?' Max asked.

'Why do you want to know?'

Max didn't answer.

'It's a long story,' the priest said.

'I have time.'

'Very well,' the priest said, and he stopped for a minute. Then he started to talk. 'I was fifteen years old. I went shopping one day with my parents and eight-year-old sister, Joanne. She was beautiful. A car came very quickly when we walked across the street. The car didn't stop and it hit my mother, father and Joanne. They all died in hospital.'

The priest started to turn again.

'No,' Max said. 'Don't move. Finish your story.'

'I was very angry and I didn't want to talk to anyone,' the priest said. 'I walked around the town. Day and night I walked. I just walked. I was angry, but I didn't know what to do. One night I came to a church. I went in and sat down. It was quiet and dark. I sat there for hours. No one came in. There was only me. And then, I heard a voice. It was my mother. She said, "Don't be angry now, Max. Don't be angry. You're at home now." That was all. I looked around me. There was no one there. I felt . . . I didn't feel angry. I felt good. I was at home. And so I became a priest.'

Max stood up and started to walk towards the door.

'Why did you come here?' the priest asked, turning in his seat. 'Why did you ask me this question? Who are you?'

Max stopped. He didn't turn around.

'My parents and sister also died when a car hit them. And I was angry. Very angry. I went to the driver's house one night and killed him.'

'How did you feel?' the priest asked.

'I felt good,' Max replied. 'I felt really good. And I didn't feel angry after that.'

'And how do you feel now?' the priest asked.

'Now I don't feel so good. I feel tired and I feel sick. But it's too late. It's too late. Goodbye.'

'Wait!' the priest said and stood up. He started to walk up to Max.

'Stop!' Max said. The priest stopped.

'Why did you come here tonight?' asked the priest.

'I wanted to know why you and I are different,' Max replied.

'Why we're different? I don't understand,' the priest said.

'No? I think I want to be like you. I just want to be like you. I'm not happy being me. But it's too late.'

'It's never too late to change,' the priest said.

Chapter 12   *You decide*

Max stood outside house number nine and looked up and down the street. There was no one there. He looked at the house – there was a light on. He moved closer to the door and could hear someone inside. Max thought of the priest's words, 'It's never too late to change.' Then he turned and started to walk away from the house. But then he thought of Fairhead and said to himself, 'I must tell the woman.'

Max walked back to the house. The light was out now. He put his hand on the door and it opened slowly. He looked inside and went in.

He didn't hear the noise behind him. He didn't see Fairhead with the gun in his hand. Fairhead hit him on the head with the gun. Max fell to the floor.

When he opened his eyes again the light was on. He tried to stand up but then stopped. A woman sat in a chair in front of him. Max was on his knees. He looked up at the woman, looked at her face.

'You!' Max said. 'I know you. But how can you be here? You're dead. I killed you. I pushed you in front of the train. You are dead.'

'Max.' It was Fairhead. He had the gun in his hand. 'You can see she's not dead. This isn't the same woman, Max. This is my daughter, Julie.'

'I don't understand.'

'We're in a parallel world, Max. You pushed a different Julie under a train in your world.'

'But why did you bring me here then?' Max shouted. 'What are you going to do with me? Do you want to kill me? Why? That wasn't your daughter! That was in *my* world!'

'Yes, Max. But you see we're all in a big family. We live in different worlds, but we're like a family. The Julies, the Maxes, the Geralds, they're different people, but they're also one person. When a Julie, Max or Gerald in one world feels something, then the Julies, Maxes and Geralds in the other worlds feel it too. When the Julie in your world is afraid, the Julie in my world also feels afraid. Do you understand? We can feel what the other person feels. When you pushed the Julie in your world under the train, the Julie in my world felt her die. And that feeling doesn't go away. It never leaves us. Julie still can't sleep at night because she feels afraid. Do you understand? Can you understand that? The Julie in your world died. But my Julie still feels afraid. Because of you. Because of what you did.'

Fairhead stopped. 'Do you understand?' he asked.

'Yes,' Max answered. 'I understand, but I'm sorry. I didn't know. I'm sorry I killed her. I'm sorry I killed all of them. I want to change, I want to be different. I can change! I came here to tell Julie about you. I didn't come here to kill her. I came to tell her about you! You must understand me. Don't kill me! Not now!'

'You want to change?' Fairhead asked. 'People like you don't change. You just don't want to die.'

'Dad, we can't do this,' said Julie.

'He came here to kill you, Julie. He kills people. It's his job. He kills people for money. He killed the Julie in his world.'

'Yes, but we're not killers.' Julie said. 'We're not him, Dad. We can't do this!'

Fairhead looked at Max. 'It's too late to change, Max.'

Max looked up at Fairhead and then slowly he stood up. 'You have the gun. You decide. Are you going to kill me? You decide. Here and now, in front of your daughter. You decide what kind of world you want to live in; what kind of world she's going to live in. You decide.'

Chapter 13 *A candle in the dark*

The priest stood near the door of the church with a candle in his hand. All at once he felt afraid. The candle fell from his hand and he fell to his knees. He heard a voice in his head. 'I'm sorry I killed her. I'm sorry I killed all of them. I want to change, I want to be different.'

The priest put his head in his hands. 'I don't want to die.'

Then all at once, he wasn't afraid. He felt good. He stood up and looked around him. There was no one in the church. He took the candle and lit it. He lit a candle in the dark church.